Kitchen Rules

Wil Spencer

Contents

Kitchen Rules

Cooking in the kitchen can be fun. But cooking can also be dangerous. Rules can help make the kitchen a safer place.

Tie your hair back or wear a hat.

Your hair may be carrying germs. A hair tie or hat will keep your hair away from the food.

Wash your hands.

Your hands may also carry germs.
Clean hands will keep the food free
from germs.

5

When You Are Cooking

Ask an adult to cut things.

Knives are very sharp.
Adults know how to handle
knives safely.

Ask an adult to handle hot things on the stove or in the oven.

Hot things can cause burns.
Adults know how to use the stove or oven without getting hurt.

Wipe up spills on the floor.

Spills can make the floor slippery. Wiping up spills right away will keep people from slipping.

Turn off the stove or oven.

If the stove or oven is left on,
it could start a fire.
Always turn the stove or oven off.

9

Clean up the kitchen.

When you are finished cooking, wipe the benches and sweep the floor. This will keep the kitchen clean.

Follow these rules when you cook.
They will help make the kitchen
a safer place.